# Lions
## in DANGER

## by Helen Orme

Consultant: Tricia Holford
The Born Free Foundation

# BEARPORT
### PUBLISHING

New York, New York

**Credits**

© age fotostock / Superstock: 5. Digital Vision: 4, 6–7, 8–9, 10–11, 12–13, 14–15, 20–21, 22–23, 25, 26–27, 28–29, 30–31, 32. Nature Picture Library: 16–17, 18–19. Every effort has been made to trace the copyright holders, and we apologize in advance for any unintentional omissions. We would be pleased to insert the appropriate acknowledgments in any subsequent edition of this publication.

*Library of Congress Cataloging-in-Publication Data*

Orme, Helen.
  Lions in danger / by Helen Orme.
      p. cm. — (Wildlife survival)
  Includes bibliographical references and index.
  ISBN-13: 978-1-59716-262-3 (library binding)
  ISBN-10: 1-59716-262-0 (library binding)
  ISBN-13: 978-1-59716-290-6 (pbk.)
  ISBN-10: 1-59716-290-6 (pbk.)
  1. Lions—Juvenile literature.  I. Title. II. Series.

  QL737.C23O76 2007
  599.757—dc22

                              2006012271

For more information, write to Bearport Publishing Company, Inc., 101 Fifth Avenue, Suite 6R, New York, New York 10003. Printed in the United States of America.

10 9 8 7 6 5 4 3 2 1

The Wildlife Survival series was originally developed by ticktock Media Ltd.

# Table of Contents

# The Grasslands

Many animals live on the **grasslands** of Africa. Some, such as antelopes, zebras, and giraffes, eat plants. Others, such as cheetahs and leopards, hunt for animals to eat. Out of all the grassland animals, however, no **predator** is as large and powerful as the lion.

A male lion's roar can be heard from about five miles (8 km) away!

# The Pride

A family of lions is called a pride. The pride often has many female lions. A female lion is called a lioness. There are only about one to four males that live with the family.

When the males are between two and four years old, they leave the pride. Sometimes they stay together in male groups. When they're old enough, however, they'll look for a pride of their own.

A pride can be made up of 3 to 50 lions.

# Male Lions

Adult males are in charge of the pride. They protect their family by roaring loudly to warn other lions to stay away. They guard the family's **territory** by leaving their scent on trees and rocks. A male lion remains leader of his pride until a younger and healthier lion fights him and takes over.

Lions have black hair at the end of their tails.

# Lion Cubs

A lioness has two to four cubs at a time. She gives birth in a **den**. This area is hidden away to keep the mother and her babies safe. Once the cubs are born, all the females in the pride look after them.

After about six weeks, cubs start to eat meat caught by their mother. They will also feed on their mother's milk until they are about six months old.

A lioness carries cubs in her mouth.

# Hunting for Food

Lions can hunt at any time of the day. However, they prefer to hunt at night.

Lionesses do most of the hunting. They are faster than male lions, which are too big and heavy to run quickly.

To get food, lions sometimes look for animals that have died or have been killed by another predator. This kind of hunting is called **scavenging**.

Lions can see in the dark six times better than humans!

# Making Way for People

Life is becoming tougher for the lions in Africa. People have started to take away their **habitat**. Some of these people are miners. They are looking for **minerals** and metals in the ground. Large areas of the grasslands have been **polluted** or destroyed by mining.

Miners often see lions as a danger to their safety. They have shot and killed the animals when they have felt threatened.

# Lions and Farmers

In the African countries where lions live, human **populations** are growing. Towns are spreading out, and more and more of the grasslands are becoming farmland.

Without the grasslands, animals such as zebras and antelopes will disappear. Hungry lions will be forced to attack livestock if they have no **prey** to hunt in the wild. Many lions are shot and killed by farmers who are trying to protect their cattle.

In some areas in Africa, people have started programs to protect both the lions and the livestock.

# The Asiatic Lion

The Asiatic lion, a cousin of the African lion, is also in danger. About 200 years ago, these animals were found from India all the way to Europe. Due to hunting and habitat destruction, there are less than 300 of them left in the world. The only place they live in the wild is in Gir National Park in India.

Asiatic lions are not as big as the African lions. The males also have smaller **manes**.

# A Safe Home

The best way to protect the lions' future is to find them a safe place to live. In Africa, some countries have set up **wildlife reserves**. In these areas, it is against the law to hunt animals.

**Wardens** help protect the lions. They also make sure that there are enough grasslands to feed the lions' prey.

Lions are often brought into the reserves from places where they are not safe.

# Do Lions Have a Future?

One way to save the lions is to bring **tourists** into the wildlife reserves. When people spend money visiting the lions, it creates jobs for those who live nearby.

Visitors, however, must be careful. They shouldn't get too close to the lions or disturb them.

For lions to survive, they must be protected. If everyone works together, lions will have a very long future.

In the wild, male lions live for 12 to 16 years, while lionesses live for 15 to 18 years.

# Just the Facts

## Where Do Lions Live?

- The red areas on the map show where African lions live.

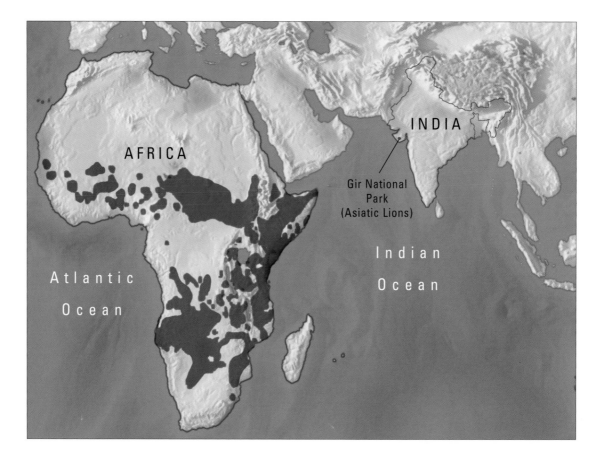

- There are many animals that live on the grasslands. Some of the predators are leopards, cheetahs, and hyenas. Some of the prey are buffaloes, wildebeests, antelopes, giraffes, zebras, and warthogs.

# Lion Bodies

A mane helps protect a male lion during a fight.
It also makes him look big and scary to other males.

**Male**
Weight: up to 529 pounds (240 kg)
Length: up to 10 feet (3 m),
including the tail

**Female**
Weight: up to 397 pounds (180 kg)
Length: up to 8.2 feet (2.5 m),
including the tail

## More About Lion Food

- Lions are **carnivores**. They hunt using teamwork so they can catch large animals, such as buffaloes. Sometimes lions eat other predators.

- Lions are not as fast as other types of big cats, such as leopards and tigers. They rely on their strength to catch and kill prey.

- While female lions do most of the hunting, the male lions get first pick of the food.

- Sometimes catching enough food is hard for lions. They rest for about 20 hours a day to save energy.

### Grasslands Food Web

This food web shows how the animals living on the African grasslands depend on plants and other animals for food. Zebras, antelopes, and giraffes eat the plants. Then they become food for the predators. The arrows in the web mean "are food for."

CHEETAHS
LEOPARDS
HYENAS
ANTELOPES
LIONS
GIRAFFES
TREES AND BUSHES
GRASSES
ZEBRAS

# More About Lion Cubs

- Cubs weigh just 2 to 4 pounds (1 to 2 kg) when they are born.

- Cubs open their eyes when they are 3 days old.

- At about 10 days old, cubs begin to walk. After about a month, they are able to run. At about this time, cubs leave the den and join the pride.

- Cubs are born with light spots or stripes on their coats. When they are about 3 months old, these start to fade away.

- When a new male lion takes over a pride, he often kills the cubs of the last male.

## More About Lions in Danger

- Between 17,000 and 23,000 wild lions live in Africa—half as many as 50 years ago.

- In some parts of Africa, lions are still hunted for sport. Hunters kill the animals, especially the males, so that they can have a dead lion as a **trophy**.

- Sometimes lions are trapped in cages and hunters are allowed to shoot them. This "canned hunting" is very cruel because the lions have no chance to escape.

# Conservation

- **Conservation** groups and governments have set up wildlife reserves for lions and their prey. These areas are protected from destruction by humans.

- Wildlife reserves are good for the local people as well as the plants and animals. If the reserves give people jobs, they will want to look after the animals.

- People are encouraged to visit the lions to help create more jobs. Most tourists take car tours of the reserves. Some reserves even allow people to mountain bike through them.

- Sometimes big cats, such as lions and leopards, are kept in poorly run zoos or circuses. Conservation groups try to rescue these animals. They find them new homes in special wildlife reserves where they can be protected.

# How to Help

Conservation is everyone's job. There are many ways to help lions:

- Learn more about lions. Then teach others at school about the importance of helping them.

- Help an organization, such as the African Wildlife Foundation (AWF) (www.awf.org). Groups such as this one raise money to pay for conservation work. To help the AWF or another conservation group, have a yard sale. Sell old clothes, toys, and books. Then donate the money that is made to the group.

- Ask your teacher if your class can adopt a lion. (Don't worry, it won't live in your classroom.) Go to a reliable Web site, such as shop.awf.org/adopt/, and see how to adopt a baby cub or a pride of lions.

*Visit these Web sites for more information on lions and how to help them:*

www.african-lion.org

www.awf.org/wildlives/148

www.pbs.org/wnet/nature/
vanishinglions/savingthelion.html#

# Glossary

**carnivores** (KAR-nuh-vorz) animals that eat meat

**conservation** (*kon*-sur-VAY-shuhn) the protection of wildlife, forests, and natural resources

**den** (DEN) an animal's home, or a hidden place where an animal sleeps or has its babies

**grasslands** (GRASS-landz) dry areas covered with grass where only a few bushes and trees grow

**habitat** (HAB-uh-*tat*) a place in the wild where an animal or plant lives

**manes** (MAYNZ) the long hairs around the neck of male lions

**minerals** (MIN-ur-uhlz) substances, such as gold, found in the earth

**polluted** (puh-LOOT-id) made dirty by chemicals, oil, or garbage that has been produced by humans

**populations** (*pop*-yuh-LAY-shuhnz) the total number of people who live in an area

**predator** (PRED-uh-tur) an animal that lives by killing and eating other animals

**prey** (PRAY) animals that are hunted by other animals for food

**scavenging** (SKAV-uhn-jing) looking for meat that other predators have left, or meat from animals that are already dead

**territory** (TER-uh-*tor*-ee) the area that belongs to an animal

**tourists** (TOOR-ists) people who are traveling on vacation

**trophy** (TROH-fee) a prize

**wardens** (WAHRD-uhnz) people whose job it is to look after protected reserves and the animals that live there

**wildlife reserves** (WILDE-life ri-ZURVZ) areas set aside, by law, for animals and plants to live in safely

# Index